Poems by

Elsie Johnstone

Selected poems

by

Elsie (Allen) Johnstone

Lakes Entrance girl

Copyright © 2020 by Elsie Johnstone

978-0-6488619-2-8

Published by G. & E. Johnstone. All rights reserved. No part of this publication may be reproduced in any manner whatsoever, or stored in a retrieval system or transmitted in any form or by any means, electronic, mechanical, photocopying, recording or otherwise, without the prior written permission of the author, except in the case of brief quotations embodied in critical articles or reviews. Please do not participate in or encourage the piracy of copyrighted materials in violation of authors' rights. Purchase only authorized editions.

The publisher and author assume no responsibility or liability whatsoever on the behalf of any purchaser or reader of this material. Any perceived slight of specific people or organizations is unintentional. While all attempts have been made to verify information provided in this publication, neither the author nor the publisher assumes any responsibility for errors, omissions or contrary interpretation of the subject matter herein.

Lakes Entrance girl is also available as an e-book for Kindle, Kobo, Apple and other devices.

Cover Picture: The Ninety Mile Beach at Lakes Entrance. Attribution: Ronidong

ACKNOWLEDGEMENTS

2020 has been a topsy-turvy year of the coronavirus, where the whole world as we know it has been turned upside down and inside out. All the ordinary things have become extraordinary and suddenly we find ourselves in lockdown. What to do?

For a writer there are many times when life is solitary, when it is just you, your thoughts and the computer. So my husband and I decided that in this time of social isolation, we would do what we do - that instead of cleaning the cupboards, shredding all our old files, or baking items made with sourdough, we would clean up our computer desktop, collect long forgotten poems and collate them into anthologies.

Over the years I have enjoyed writing poems as a mental exercise, an emotional outlet, a search for understanding. As I perused my catalogue, I realised that many of them have been penned about my old girlhood hometown, Lakes Entrance, so this first compilation is about the East Gippsland fishing village and my connections there. I am calling it, *Lakes Entrance girl*, a poetic follow-up to earlier books, *Our Little Town - Growing up in Lakes Entrance*, a compilation of oral histories across the generations, and *Around the Kitchen Table*, stories, yarns and poems from the old days.

Thank you Lakes Entrance and the people of my childhood for being such a magical place to grow, a place where nothing mattered except what went on in the neighbourhood and the people who inhabited it.

I wisely chose wonderful parents. They were good, kind and generous people. Thank you Jack and Theresa Allen, now deceased, who shared everything they had, and imparted a sense of trust, love, morality and optimism. Childhood experiences provide a canvas for life and I was granted a colourful and sweeping brush.

I am number two of ten children, all of us different. We have rubbed against and moulded each other, sharing parents, experiences, celebrations and sorrows. So, Margaret (dec), Joan, Kathleen, John (dec), Maureen, Arthur, Mary, Eileen and Robert (dec), I thank you for being 'my mob'. I have loved and appreciated you all, and you have enriched my life.

In turn, our children chose us and we are grateful. Caitlin, Tessa, Chris and Eloise, what a great crew you turned out to be, embracing life with energy and imagination, giving us eleven fantastic grandchildren, embracing us as adults, allowing us to share in your dreams and nightmares.

And to our eleven grandchildren? What can I say? You are all different and you are all magnificent. Embrace the world, believe in yourselves and have enjoyable lives. Life is for living.

To my husband, life partner and mentor of nearly fifty years, Graeme Johnstone. Thank you, I have loved growing old with you. How lucky am I?

Before we start…

THIS BLOODY VIRUS

My world has been turned upside down
I've been stood on my head and swirled round and round
Yesterday the world was mine for the taking
I could go anywhere and see who I wanted
Conduct my life without being taunted
If I did that now, new laws I'd be breaking.
How can it happen so quickly?
Surely a virus can't make you so sickly
And threaten us all
If one should fall
It has a domino effect
The virus will run rampage if not severely checked.
The pollies and medicine men have their say
Stay inside, don't go out today
Unless it's for food, medicine or exercise
Stay home lest you compromise
Your health or that of your neighbour
Stay at home until we can immunise
That's the one thing that will be our saviour
This won't be over 'til it's over

CONTENTS

Introduction 1
My home town 3
Jemmy's Point 4
The old fisherman 5
The Ninety Mile Beach 6
Gippsland Lakes 7
Nowa Nowa 8
The day the sea broke through 9
Carmel, our old home 10
Up the lake in the boat 12
Camping 14
The liquidambar 15
Girlfriends 16
This child 17
Empty nest 18
A tin full of photos 19
Comfort zone 20
Margaret Anne 22
Theresa Mary 24
My brother John 26
Robert Desmond 27
Jack's story 28
Call waiting 31
Aileen 32
Arthur Moffatt 34
The local football team 35
Change 36
History 37
If the internet broke 38
A cure for loneliness 39
The veranda 40
Every person has a story 42
Grandmother 43
We're all dying to go there 44
Time to end the isolation 45
Other books by Elsie Johnstone 47

LAKES ENTRANCE GIRL

POEMS ABOUT LAKES ENTRANCE AND GIPPSLAND

I lived in Lakes Entrance for the first seventeen years of my life before I left for education and work, but the place has had a profound effect on me. For me, there is no place quite so beautiful, tranquil, alluring.

We have maintained a holiday cottage on the hill at Lakes overlooking the ocean, which is our retreat to escape the busyness of every-day life. For over fifty years we have returned regularly to engage with family and because we love it. This glorious part of Gippsland has changed much in that time but one constant remains. It is still so beautiful, tranquil, alluring.

I love the sound of the ocean, the brisk sea breezes, the Milky Way at night and the chill mist in the morning, the smell of salt water, the waterbirds flying home to roost in the evening.

I love the beauty that can take your breath away, that although familiar, is always changing.

I love the heartbeat of the town - slow and quiet in winter, bright and sparkly in summer.

I love the fishing village atmosphere and fresh fish and prawns that can be bought straight from the boats. We take them home, cook them up, and open a bottle of wine, while we sit on the deck and watch the sun set over the sea.

Lakes Entrance shaped me and influenced many of my life choices - the country boy I married, my home by the water, the sports I follow, the food I cook, the art I enjoy, the books I read, the places I travel. My children holidayed there and they now bring their children to enjoy the surf, the sand, the bush and the ice cream.

I have travelled the world, been on every continent, seen many awe-inspiring sights but I will never take for granted the instant when the car draws over the hill at Kalimna and the sea and lakes in all their glory are unwrapped before me, their beauty taking my breath away.

As they say, 'You can take the girl out of Lakes Entrance but you can't take Lakes Entrance out of the girl.'

I am a Lakes Entrance girl.

- *Elsie (Allen) Johnstone*

LAKES ENTRANCE GIRL

MY HOME TOWN

It's funny how a place can draw you to it
It's just a place, you understand and know it
But it's my place, the place that bore and grew me
The place when I was young that everybody knew me
Is it the place, so pretty and picturesque
Or the people in it that I love the best?
Perhaps it's something deep down in my psyche
That ties me to the place and makes it likely
That I will return again and again
If not in reality then often in my dreams
It's really difficult to explain
I left there long ago but it seems
The ocean waves and still backwater
Take me back to when I was a young daughter
And with my sisters roamed the swamps and dunes
The salty backdrop of fancy-free afternoons
Seagulls squawked and swans in unison soared high
A child's weather forecast in the sky, 'Wet, dry, wet, dry, wet, dry'
Chilled sea air permeated the atmosphere as the returning fleet
Crossed the bar, and the town's children rushed to the jetties to greet
Their fathers, returning from a day working at sea
Is it feast? Or famine? What will it be?

JEMMY'S POINT

Down in East Gippsland
Where the lakes flow to the sea
There's a lookout place where fishermen
Judge what the weather will be
Before they venture out, they must first decide
What sort of conditions lie ahead, how strong is the tide?
Can the trusty trawler breach the dangerous sandy bar
Where foam and wild waves crash and churn like an avatar?
Can the little fishing boat navigate the swell?
Will she be able to go out to sea and get back home as well?
Will the fish be schooling in a favourite fishing spot?
Or will it be a waste of fuel and a catch that comes to nought?
All these things fishermen think and talk about
Gazing to the horizon from Jemmy's Point Lookout
But the major talking point that's on everybody's mind
Is, on Saturday, can the boys play well enough to defeat the bastards
down the line?

LAKES ENTRANCE GIRL

THE OLD FISHERMAN

The old fisherman can't keep away from the sea
He tells tales of adventures and how things used to be
How when the weather was bad, he mended his nets
As he chatted with others about footy and bets
And when that was done, he'd fill up a barrel
And tan them by boiling up bark from the wattle
The sea was his ally, his partner, his nemesis
It was also his master, he could ill afford arrogance
He studied its moods, and therefore he knew
That it could turn angry when the south wind blew
He remembered the times when the waves were so high
His trawler in the gully could not see the sky
The elements could take his sturdy old boat
Toss it and roll it, make it a scapegoat
For the awful abuse that it had to abide
When flotsam and jetsam washed in with the tide
Life wasn't easy but like all old salts
He cherished his trade with all of its faults
The thrill of navigating the surging breakwater
On heavy haul days, his boat low in the water
Because of the catch he had gathered at sea
Knowing how happy his home folk would be
As he headed towards port with his catch for the day
Overhead, pelicans and sea birds heralded the way
For his trusty old trawler with its idiosyncrasies
Which provided for him and his family's families
The old fisherman reflects as he looks out to the sea
What a great life his has turned out to be
How grateful was he that life dealt him his hand
Of a seafaring life, 'stead of life on the land

THE NINETY MILE BEACH

Golden beach
Chilled sea mist
Where Bass Strait meets Southern Ocean
Dolphins and seabirds in harmonic motion
Waves stand tall in high command
Crash, smash, froth in and out
Seashells discarded on golden sand
Washed, sloshed, tossed about
Flung back and forth to the shore
Home to crustaceans no more
A surfer's thong rides like a boat
A child's red bucket by the moat
Of a sandcastle built in the sand
A whole sand village, a wonderland
Little blue soldier crabs scurry
To their holes, in a hurry
Escape unseen to their mezzanine
Before the next wave crashes in
To the left and right as far as one sees
A gold highway, gritty and pristine
Endless sand, no grass, no trees
Where pelicans play and gulls convene
The Ninety Mile Beach is ours to treasure
Let's endeavour to join together
To preserve her as she is forever

GIPPSLAND LAKES

This land of nature not of man
Mere creatures in a master plan
Rolling hills where rivers wake
Drift to the sea via creek and lake
Mighty rivers flow
Stiff southern winds blow
Until it calms to ne'er a quiver
Dense stillness, morning on the river
Then once more upon the morrow
Begins the dance of joy and sorrow
Fluffy whites scuttle 'cross the sky
Streamers in the wind streaking by
Sometimes hanging deep and dark
Threatening, omnificent, stark
Until at night they fade and die
Replaced by bright holes in the sky
Hanging low, soft lanterns glow
For sailors, navigating where to go
Stars showing a milky way
To avoid the crags in sea's highway
At dawn, calm pink glory
As sun heralds another day, another story

NOWA NOWA

On the way to Orbost
By the turn-off to Buchan and Omeo
There's a delightful little hamlet
That not many people know
A pristine fresh stream bubbles
Over boulders and stony ground
The tinkle of the bellbird, the only breaking sound
That rings gently in the whispering breeze
Of majestic old, grey gumtrees
The shy heath blushes and bold gold wattles bloom
Along the modest avenue to the quaint school room
Where children have learnt their lessons and happily played
As their dads in the forest plied their noisy daytime trade
Doing tough men's work, they needed to be strong
To work in local timber mills and in the bush beyond
On the other side of the highway, a truly wondrous place
The home land of Kurnai people of the ancient aboriginal race
A piece of paradise on earth
Assigned to them by God at birth
Sustaining them for eons before settlers came
With bountiful grains and fish and a multitude of game
When white man arrived, he left nothing on the shelf
Took Kurnai country and used it for himself
Failed to acknowledge or try to understand
Banished the native people from their home land
The two cultures collided
For many years remained divided
Whiteman, bogeyman, came out top man
Kurnai banished; culture almost vanished
Let's recognise that wrongs were done and the need to readjust
Meet each other on equal terms, be willing to learn to trust.

LAKES ENTRANCE GIRL

THE DAY THE SEA BROKE THROUGH

Old fishermen and our indigenous know
That every five or six years or so
At Lake Tyers there's a lake in the chain
Where the sea washes through and closes in again
They recognise signs that predict this phenomenon
And keep vigil for when this is about to happen
For it cleans the lake system and its bounty replenishes
Nourishes the environment so that sea life flourishes
A day in my life I will take to my grave
Was one such occasion where the sea surged and raved
Two metres from the lake so still and so calm
How could it be that close without doing harm?
Busy little sandpipers scampered 'cross the dunes
To the lake, all but depleted, a series of lagoons
Divided into humps and bumps that little islands made
Upon which young children a game of pirates played
Happily, engrossed in their imaginary wonderland
While eel tracks across the breach indented the damp sand
Leaving trails behind them revealing their escape
To the sea, with passion in their hearts, looking for a mate
In the deeper water, mature fish waited patiently
To be at last set free into the wide blue sea
Overhead Pacific gulls hovered in the sky
Hoping they might grab a little fishy swimming by
I was with my fisherman father, an old sea salt
Who had seen it all before, but still awe and wonder felt
That day I consider we were all so very blessed
To experience mother nature, her glory manifest

CARMEL, OUR OLD HOME

On the valuable block in the centre of town
Old house, doomed for knock down
Empty, desolate, forsaken, alone
No sound of a clock, no ring of a phone
No laugh of a child, no television roaring
Bushes grown up, white ants boring
Its walls hold tales of another time
When life was more simple, people more kind
The parents cleaned and polished and swept
Tended the garden and made sure they kept
Home in good order for the family they grew
They made it so cosy, the kids all loved it too
They had parties, gatherings, barbeques, family dos,
Every inch of the house put to good use
But the children they grew and dispersed from the block
To travel and marry, depart from their flock
The parents grew old and feeble and died
The children came home, remembered and cried
The house was redundant; they had homes of their own
It was just a nuisance, with lawns to be mown
A word with an auctioneer, quick campaign and 'Yours, sir'
Not worth preserving, must think of the purse, sir
Knock it down, develop, that's the mentality

LAKES ENTRANCE GIRL

In this day and age, no sentimentality
The moneyman pondered, measured and planned
He could turn good profit just from this land
But then came a saviour with love in his heart
All this old place needs, is a good upward tart
This fine old home, lying empty, alone
Will shelter my family until they are grown
With lots of hard work and dirt on my hands
I can return her to former glory just as she stands
She'll not be knocked down and her history dismantled
Instead we'll restore her so she's spruce and newfangled
Her bones are good, she stands tall and straight
We'll plaster the walls and paint the front gate
Once again, she'll be grand and warm and secure
Happy voices, small children like families before

UP THE LAKE IN THE BOAT

Sunday was a rest from work and activity
A day for church, roast dinner and festivity
The town was silent, the fishing boats were in
This day was for family fun, ice creams, a swim
In the rolling surf water of the Ninety Mile Beach
And for families where motor cars were not beyond reach
A drive out into the bush with picnic and chainsaw
No matter how much wood you had, you could still do with more!
Our family's mode of transport was our trusty family boat
She wasn't grand, she wasn't flash, but we thought her best afloat
She was our sail to freedom, the Erin was her name
She served the family very well, a truly grand old dame
She had been in the family since the turn of the century
Tended and cared for by generations of our ancestry
During the week she earned her keep, diligent in her wake
And come Sunday she'd be put to work to take us up the lake
The family would all jump aboard, the family dog in tow
Start her up, 'Tut, tut, tut,' now where would you like to go?
Out of the Backwater, under the bridge, into the channel wide

LAKES ENTRANCE GIRL

To the Barrier, the New Works, perhaps over the West Side,
Maybe to Nyerimilang, Nungurner, Metung or Box's Creek
A whole day out in Paynesville, the highlight of the week
Pull in to Rigby Island, boil up the blackened billy
Pass the sandwiches around, along with sweet, hot tea
So many, many outings, but the one I loved best by far
Was when we turned the bow around to head up the North Arm
Out beyond folks' houses scattered on the hill
Into a wonderland where place and time stood still
The only sign of settlement was where creek became a stream
And old Mrs Comer ran a teahouse, serving hot scones,
jam and cream
She'd spot the boat, take her apron off and come down for a chat
Discussing news from round the town, canvassing this and that
While the grown ups talked and laughed, we kids would go explore
As far as we were allowed to go along the muddy shore
Pretend to be, aborigine, who walked this land for centuries
And had the dreamtime stories etched deep in their memories
As I look back now, how privileged were we
To be brought up amid this unspoilt tranquillity.

CAMPING

Ninety Mile Beach on a long summer's day
Lay back, read a book, watch children play
Wild surf pounding onto sandy shore
Bodies tossed and plunging, always going back for more
Games of cricket on the sand
Dancing the night away to a band
Sitting round the campsite waiting to be fed
Sizzling sausages and red sauce on white bread
Card games after dinner, perhaps a sing-a-long
Balmy evenings stretch, making warm days long
Laying on a camp bed, weary bodies emitting heat
Reliving the ocean's rhythm
Where sleep and dreams meet
Looking forward to tomorrow when we shall repeat the same
That's just so long, of course, that it doesn't rain
Then we shall be huddling in a damp, dark tent
Playing endless card games, wondering where summer went
Watching wet soggy drips racing, threatening to invade us
Digging trenches around the tent, hoping that will save us
Trusting that the forecast squall, settles before it hits us all
And our summer camp becomes so damp
It's far too wet to stay
And sends us on our way

LAKES ENTRANCE GIRL

THE LIQUIDAMBAR

We bought our weatherboard cottage purely on a whim
We fell in love at first sight, it seemed to invite us in
And convince us that we could live happily forever in this home
We knew it could be a place where young children could be grown
We walked into the garden through the pretty little gate
And saw the liquidambar tree; that seemed to settle fate
Its branches reaching high and wide, filtering the light
We instinctively knew right there and then, this house was exactly right
The liquidambar beckoned us
In its spreading grandeur promised us
Our family could grow strong and tall
The 'ambar' would protect us all
By harvesting carbon during the day
Emitting oxygen while we slept the night away
In summer its branches are lush and green
Cooling the house, nature's own sunscreen
Sheds its leaves in autumn to enrich the soil beneath
Covering the garden paths with a magic golden sheaf
Once devoid of foliage, the winter sun shines through
Warming the coldest, dankest days, making diamonds in the dew
After the dreary winter, new buds herald the spring
Fresh leaves appear, the world is bright as new life forms within
Lush foliage provides a happy place for possum and birds to play
The joyful sounds of spring tell us that summer is on its way
The family grew and the house was enlarged
Extra bedrooms added, a study, more room in the garage
The garden evolved but the constants remain
Our liquidambar majestically stands tall, queen of her domain
On the day we bought our home, how could we have known
That the 'ambar' would care for us long after the kids have grown

GIRLFRIENDS

Friends are the bridges that help one pass
Along life's pathways, through rough stones and smooth grass
Friendship is a two-way street
A mingling of lives where certain souls meet
Two rivers joining their flowing waters
The meeting of other parents' daughters
To exist side by side through the thistles and tangle
Navigate the journey through the same jungle
It takes a long time to grow an old friend
Who has been there for you from beginning to end
Talked over problems, shared feelings and dreams
Offered counsel, support and all in-betweens
Nurtured you with love, trust, care and fun
Tended and shaded you, moved you into the sun
Friends who have known you from young girls to old ladies
Who have shared your hopes, your joys and maladies
I love my old friends, my buddies, my pals
Throughout my life they have served me so well
They have laughed and cried with me
Left me alone when I wanted to be
Played games, recipes exchanged, babies' nappies changed
As we fondly watched our young ones mature and grow
Make their own mistakes, never wanting to know what we know
I am so grateful my girlfriends walked by my side
Enjoying the trip, sign posting the ride
From optimistic young mothers who had much living to do
To contented old grannies, now nearly all the way through
A member of one's family can also be friend
But old friends are family, right through to the end

LAKES ENTRANCE GIRL

THIS CHILD

This unexpected, uninvited, unplanned parcel
A giggle, a burp, a squirm, a smile, a gargle
Precious baby to love, our family extended
Siblings rejoice, their love open ended
Once again nurturing days
Our lives expand in many ways
The love baby brings is inexplicable
The joy and comfort so predictable
New life to share with family and friends
For born again parents community expands
Infectious laughter brightens our home
This little baby is our queen on a throne
Life moves on unceremoniously
What was to be is changed irrevocably
It is not what we planned that is indisputable
But this child is delightfully ours! So beautiful!
Baby learns and grows, makes her needs understood
Always believing life is going to be very good

EMPTY NEST

Grown child leaving
Embracing career opportunity
New life, different community
Mother silently grieving
Moving day, up and away
A brave smile, a hug and a kiss
A wave goodbye, a tear in the eye
Can't wait, mustn't miss the plane
Gone!
Letting go is bitter sweet
Pride and pain
Empty time sheet
Home again
To an empty house
An old wife with her old husband
A pot of tea
Reflection, circumspection
Everywhere a memory
Feelings of rejection
Intricate mosaic torn apart
A mournful ache in her heart
Feels bereft
What is left?
But not for long
This melancholy
A whole world is there to see
Child is gone, move right on
Job is done, time for fun
Depart the past
Free at last!

LAKES ENTRANCE GIRL

A TIN FULL OF PHOTOS

When the relations came to stay
After tea, table cleared, and things put away
Out came the chocolate boxes and decorated tins
Full of family photos, family history held within
They were emptied on to the table top
Picked up, examined and then we'd swap
One for another, to examine and discover
What child was like our father and who was like our mother
We'd talk about who was who, what he did,
and how he was related
Where we went, what we thought, old family tales debated
Photos of the old folk long since gone
Through the mist of days gone past, and in us who live on
Weddings, babies, young women in their prime
Young men dressed in uniform who fell fighting in war time
We exclaimed at the beauty of Margaret Gaul
The photo of old Aunty Jess before she had her fall
We scoffed at Aunty Lulla's wedding bonnet
A Carmen Miranda affair with fruit and flowers upon it
Talk of how Uncle Jimmy lost his teeth
while swimming in the surf
And how the boys painted the white horse black, always caused
much mirth
We retold tales of long lost cousins, eccentric aunts and balladeers
Noble, amusing and tragic things that happened over the years
These were great evenings, enjoyed by young and old
When family tales were commented upon and history was retold
Truth wasn't exactly vital; it changed at each recital
Because we knew that within the family loop
The yarn was spun for a bit of fun, just to amuse the group

COMFORT ZONE

'Get out of your comfort zone,' they say
'Why would I do that?' I pray
The comfort zone is comfortable
That's where I like to sit
It's easy to be there
I am totally at ease with it
I experience low levels of anxiety and stress
Enjoy a challenge but not a contest
Steady performance, relaxed disposition
I love my life and its anxiety-neutral position
Enough love, food, talent, time, admiration
Never striving beyond my station
Accepting of the life I have
Could be better, but it's not too bad
'Step out of your comfort zone,' others say
We are all very vulnerable
Should never be so comfortable
That we chill our lives away
Life is a series of challenges
Checks and balances

LAKES ENTRANCE GIRL

We are here to compete and train
Enjoy the surge of adrenalin to the brain
Get comfortable with being uncomfortable
Resist the urge for fight or flight, be vulnerable
Ignore basic instinct
What loved ones think
Be constantly scared so you know you're alive
Have no destination, set constant goals for you to strive
Making sure you always place them just out of reach
Life was not meant to be relaxing with a martini on a beach
Spend your whole life outside your comfort zone
That sounds a sure recipe for ending up alone
My take is the opposite of that
Step up to the plate when it's your turn to bat
Do the best that you can with all that you know
Relax, take it easy, just have a go
We are here to grow comfortably old
So sit back, relax, let life unfold

MARGARET ANNE

By 1946 the fighting had ceased
Young spirits had at last been released
From the scars of battle and politicians' strife
Returning home to the simple life
Setting aside grief for lost mates on foreign shore
And swore that there'd be no more war
They returned home, hunkered down, embraced each new day
Just glad to be free to marry, work and play
In their humble fishing town, to live and let live
Forget, maybe, not forgive
Into this world came Margaret Anne
First born of the huge Allen clan
Margaret, complex in her simplicity
Content to allow things just to be
Grew up loving the little town
Met her lover, married, settled down
Away from her town, physically
It remained within her spiritually

LAKES ENTRANCE GIRL

To seven babies she gave birth
Each one a reflection of her own worth
Life brought its share of troubles
She took refuge in baby's cuddles
Loving her home and the children reared in it
Gave to each child as they needed it
Be it a hug, encouragement, praise
Nurturing, caring, sharing, on their side always
She empathised, criticized, idolized
Fiercely protecting like a mother hen
Forever watching over them
Her family was her currency
She fought for them 'til eternity
God help those who stood on her toe
Or stuck a nose where it should not go
The children grew and left their home
Had precious babies of their own
She so dearly loved them all
Eagerly awaiting each phone call
To the mum they loved, admired, respected
Separated by life but still connected
She returned to live in her little town
Happy to be home where she'd been grown
We miss dear Margaret Anne, our Margaret Anne
First-born of the unwieldy Allen clan

THERESA MARY

My doctor announced to me late last week
That my life had derailed, treatment had failed
'All over Red Rover,' the verdict
I listened, accepted, I heard it
The Angel of Death is coming my way
Please don't be so sad, I know how to pray
My life will be over before the week's end
No more we can do, let's not pretend
At eighty-five years I've been around for a bit
You never think that this will come to it
My struggle is over so I take to my bed
Into which, in my prime I fell exhausted and spent
My refuge, a place where I lay my head
To awake early each morning refreshed and alive
With the man that I wed by my side
So busy, no time for discontent
By the rhythm of nature I lived all my life
Embraced each new challenge every day
I was content to be a good mother and wife
My love and I sustained each other that way
By a different name I go to God, the dying and birthing me
Nevertheless, I am whom I am inside
Only sisters know how I used to be
A unique essence who laughed, dreamed and cried
The quintessential me
Old friends hold reminiscences, ours alone to compare
My dying confronts them because they really care
Word spread I was dying so all week they came
To sit by my side, hold my hand, say goodbye
Pay respects, acknowledge we shared time and place
Some regretted the things they'd done and would cry
We lived in the same pond, our own special space

LAKES ENTRANCE GIRL

A few were glad that with my passing
To life everlasting
Old hurts would be forgotten
Old debts released
Old grudges abandoned
Old quarrels appeased
A few grateful souls come to thank me
For some good deed they still feel indebted
Lent an ear, paid a visit, made them welcome to tea
Some small kindness, comforted a sick child that fretted
But the ones I love best are those other old women
All so busy with their own lives
We barely had time to socialize
Each so different from me
But one thing we had in common
We strove for our community
Took every opportunity
To make our town a better place
To live and grow
We tried our best, that I know
I shared a common experience these other wives
My sisters in time, we lived parallel lives
The clock continues to tick, time is finite
We can't live forever, that is not our birthright
Time on earth has elapsed, and there is no more trying
Like the journey from my mother's womb
I will not remember my own dying
In that nanosecond between life and the tomb
The ultimate truth becomes apparent
My life was defined by being a parent
In the genetic imprint I leave behind
My immortality is defined

MY BROTHER JOHN

My brother John was a damn good bloke
Who proudly wore his priestly cloak
With dignity and generosity
Viewed by some with curiosity
Connected but separated
Loved, applauded and berated
Sometimes even hated
Because evil men had betrayed holy trust
Committed crimes beyond disgust
Good priests like John shouldered the blame
They were, without distinction, judged the same
For the sin of abusement
And sexual amusement
Where children were sacrificed
All in the name of Christ
How my heart bleeds for good men like John
Who did so much good and were so wronged
His trust in his Church was so betrayed
It drove him to an early grave
His congregation horrified
Bucketsful of tears were cried
The sad, sad day our John died

LAKES ENTRANCE GIRL

ROBERT DESMOND

Son, sibling, uncle, friend
Adored yet rejected
His life choices disrespected
A broken heart that couldn't mend
Avid collector
People connector
Robert loved Abba, Dolly, Kylie and Queen
And all the old stars of the silver screen
He enjoyed the royal family
And all sorts of ceremony
He was great fun, great company
The girls all loved him, he was safe to be with, you see
But the love of his life was Roger, his partner
They shared their lives, their tears, toil and laughter
Walking side by side along life's rocky journey
Supporting each other, standing together, strong and firmly
Robert, a dear kind soul, a broken-hearted clown
Who kept the dark secret of how he'd been let down
His whole life ruined before he was grown
He suffered in silence, afraid and alone
Burying deep inside him the shocking abuse
While doing his best to entertain and amuse
He died prematurely; it was too much for him to bear
Leaving us asking, how could we have been there
For our shiny, glittery jewel, larger-than-life brother?
One of a kind, unlike any other

JACK'S STORY

Mother left us
Bereft us
No longer by our sides
To shower us with love and affection
We drift on foreign tides
Swirling in unknown directions
As two children mortality face
A disconnected pair
In a very scary place
United in the grief we share
Alone but together
On our boat in stormy weather
Father came to school that day
Eyes swollen and red, face grey
Our strong fisherman father crying
Awkward and shocked about her dying
Taking small boys' hands in large calloused ones
'Your mother is dead,' he blurted to his sons
Walked us the long walk home
Confused, together but still alone
Father floated aboard his own nightmare
Too much grief to share or care
That his two boys needed him there
Found solace in the pub
The tough fishermen's club

LAKES ENTRANCE GIRL

Dulled emotions with alcoholic potions
In his lonely house we cried
Washed ashore, tossed by tide
Shipwrecked, cast aside
Eighty odd years I walked this earth
From the day of my birth
Yet, still I cry tears of despair
Of how mother died and left me here
My Mother, my significant other
I shut my eyes and hear her say
'I love you, son, I'm going away
'Say your prayers and love your God
'I will always walk by your side'
Then Father's yellow shadow in a hospital bed
His arteries hardened, his liver bled
Wartime bureaucracy granted compassionate leave
Once again, time to grieve
What does a nineteen-year-old know
About mending bridges from long ago?
My father dead from drink, broken hearted
His two sons carry his casket
Lay it to rest for eternity
Disappointed with his paternity
I continued living, rarely speaking his name
Childhood hurts locked deep within
Heart hardened by rejection pain
Never forgiving his sin
Of omission, no contrition
As life progressed, I gradually related more
To the man who had gone before
I learnt to empathize
Not chastise

I married my love and felt complete
Faded photos from my parents' wedding day
Did their union feel this way?
My children brought such joy and pride
Did my father feel the same inside?
At thirty-five years in my physical prime
The same age as my father when his wife was taken
How utterly bereft and sad the time
An empty bed in which to waken
In my father's shoes I stood and cried
Tears of sympathy
For the man who failed but tried
A litany of fragility
My attitude softens, but childhood hurts remain
Time heals
The forty-two-year-old me kneels
By a grey concrete slab inscribed and named
To my shame
With no love
He died alone prematurely
When he was the same age as me
I cry for this man who with grief so consumed
He left his two sons marooned
With their wound
After that I progressed alone
No reference, no milestone
To tie me to the man I never really knew
But I can see life now from his point of view
This issue that plagued me all my life
How we lost each other in our grief
We a mother, he his wife
It is my belief
I should have tried to understand
That this was not his plan
He'd been dealt a dud hand

CALL WAITING

We have you on hold
Don't be so bold
As to expect a person to answer your call
Instead, head to the web, which will tell you all
You would prefer to speak to a customer officer for assistance?
Please hold
Don't scold
We reward persistence for lasting the distance in this timeless existence
Thank you for waiting for us to communicate
We don't mean to aggravate
Blood pressure up, health deteriorating
This call waiting is extremely frustrating
Eyes rotate, I am about to asphyxiate
Badly need a toilet break
I've held so long I'm about to crack
These hours of my life I will never get back
Hang on grimly, surely, it's my turn soon
I made this call in the early morning
It is now late afternoon!

AILEEN

The hearse snails its solitary way
Only the priest follows
To the cemetery
Townsfolk in silent homage
Stop to pray
Who is it? Who lies dead in that cortege?
Did she live amongst us?
Aileen died
In the night
Lonely
Neither family nor friends around her
If only
We had known, we may have found her
In time
Prevented her decline
Sweet second daughter, smart, bold, daring
Pretty, strong-minded, caring
Unplanned pregnancy
Up the chute with bun in oven
Left holding the baby, bored, tired, unfulfilled
Showed no mercy

LAKES ENTRANCE GIRL

Young man responsible, not overly thrilled
Was marched up the aisle to become her husband
Reluctant groom, promised nothing
More children followed
Then tragedy
Family calamity
Torn apart
Broken heart
Deflated, self medicated
Retreated, defeated
Left at home, alone
Paths overgrown
Death's smell beckoned them through the gate
Aileen was dead, it was too late
What did she think of as she lay dying?
Alone and crying
Slow sludge winding down ancient mountain
Life ebbing from life's fountain
All alone
Should we have known?

ARTHUR MOFFATT

He wasn't the first and unfortunately won't be the last
Although it's many years since Arthur Moffatt passed
Not a lot has changed, it's still happening too often
Another black body wrapped up and placed in a coffin
In 1987, at just fifty one years old
Arthur Allen Moffatt joined that lonely fold
A victim of the system, died in captivity
The law was against him, it was ingrained bigotry
Born and raised on country at Lake Tyers Peninsula
Known to its traditional owners simply as Bung Yarnda.
The grandson of Laurie, a man much admired
The last king of the Krowathunkooloong tribe
One of five that formed the Gunaikurnai nation
Most of whom ended up on Lake Tyers Station
Ruled by bureaucrats and told how to live
Controlled and disrespected, the injustice hard to forgive
Nevertheless, his boyhood was happy and carefree
He fished, hunted and played games as was meant to be
But his life changed suddenly when on the whim of a politician
Families were pressured to leave the Lake Tyers mission
Find somewhere else to live, vacate and relocate
His family moved to Warragul, where Arthur met his final fate
He was arrested for drinking too much, for making a fuss
It wouldn't be a crime for the white ones of us
Unceremoniously detained and deprived of his liberty
He became another sad statistic for aboriginal deaths in custody

LAKES ENTRANCE GIRL

THE LOCAL FOOTBALL TEAM

I was never any part of it
But could not be unaware
Of the joy in sports that the boys could play
And girls weren't allowed to share
In the little town where I grew up
The lifeblood flowed from the football club
It was a sacred domain for men and boys
A rich source of worldly grief and joys
If the team won on a Saturday
It didn't matter what happened any other day
The mood of the town was determined, it seemed
By how well the boys gelled as a team
From selection on Thursday to the Sunday debrief
A win for the boys was such a relief
Then from Monday to Thursday the discussion transgressed
Whether this one or that one could play at his best
Was the new coach doing his job
To train, enhance skills and nurture his mob?
Would team injuries be an impediment?
Whether the young rover was arrogant
Did Spud have the right temperament?
Would the coming bye be to the team's detriment?
Should young Richo play on the forward line or at the back?
If Saturday is wet and wild should Jacko play attack?
Is Crawf a natural ruckman, is Barney best in goal?
Has the car crash Jim was in, taken its nasty toll?
The old folk celebrated the men of the current team
But it would seem
They reckoned, at the same time
They would have done much better
When they were in their prime

CHANGE

The one constant in life is change
No matter how much we rearrange
Substitute, erase, embrace
Convert, alter or replace
Try as we may with all our might
What we do is not finite
Like the wheels on a bicycle
Life is a continuing, evolving cycle
If those wheels happen to get stuck
You get thrown off the bike and into the muck

HISTORY

History is about the victor's glory
Never her story, always his story
Men went to war leaving women at home
To bare and nurture children, exist on their own
When history is written the good is accentuated
Victories are celebrated, heroes venerated
We read of bloody battles where our side prevailed,
Rarely confronted by defeats or how we have failed
While we bathe in war and promote its glories
The dark side of humanity is not part of the stories
If we delved a bit deeper no doubt, we'd discover
In the evils of war, that both sides suffer
For millennia aborigines lived in Australia
The school history we read demonstrated failure
To include them as part of the equation
Inhabiting the land before white invasion
We learnt of the explorers, honourable and brave
When in fact they took the land and its occupants enslaved
Settling it as if it was theirs for the keeping
Leaving aborigine tribes decimated and weeping
No history spoke of sons of earls, dukes and peers
Who took huge chunks of country as if it was theirs
Enslaving aborigines and keeping them captive
Whipping and jailing them if they proved maladaptive
Did the squatters have a divine right to squat
Valuing sheep and cattle more, when they were not
Terra Nullius deemed the land unoccupied
Brushed aborigines aside, their claims nullified
Thus, ensuring the British Empire survived

IF THE INTERNET BROKE

What if on-line went off-line?
Global catastrophe, big time
If the internet broke
How would we 'like' and 'share' and 'poke'?
Would friends disappear?
The world collapse in fear
How will we share our photos, organize events
Keep in touch with family and friends
Will the street burn with riots?
What will I do with my nights?
With no YouTube to make us all laugh
How will the world know when I'm drawing a bath?

A CURE FOR LONELINESS

Lonely people experiencing life through filtered lens
Talking to friends
Hundreds of them
Facebook's odds and ends
They love me, LOL
They tell me so
They laugh at jokes
Grant pokes
Socially isolated
Negated, sedated
Self-absorbed
Sad and bored
Stuff my face with comfort food
Pretending to be happy and fulfilled
Lonely people running
Shunning connection
Fearing rejection
Preening in the gym
Keeping slim
All the time searching for physical perfection
And affection
Endless activity
Diverts
Locked in captivity
It hurts
Seek social connection
Include
Don't exclude
There is difference between loneliness and solitude
Reject jog and blog
Go out and get yourself a dog

THE VERANDA

The old Australian veranda was there for all to see
A couple of comfy chairs 'side the door, a table for taking tea
Mornings in the northern sunlight, afternoons in the shade
Enjoying the peace and tranquillity while watching the passing parade
Chatting with townsfolk who happened to be strolling past
Talking about local news and after families asked
Towards the back, the veranda had trellises and potted plants
Boots lined up by the door, balls and toys askance
Perhaps a rope clothesline strung across for rainy weather
An old cane lounge and beds for pets, dogs and cats together
The veranda sheltered windows from sun on a hot Australian day
Shaded the house from baking heat, just a few feet away
On a balmy summer's evening when all the work was done
After a day of blazing heat and relentless summer sun
As the night light fell and the day's cares slowly eased
To the sound of cicadas and the kiss of the soft sea breeze
The family sat out on kitchen chairs and sipped a cup of tea
Chattered in muted tones and told tales of what used to be
Shelled peas for tomorrow as kookaburras heralded rain
And the black swans in formation headed home to the swamp again

LAKES ENTRANCE GIRL

The children played happily doing somersaults on cool grass
The parents spoke to the neighbours who happened to be going past
A veranda is a halfway house between inside and out
It connects us to the wider world, of that there can be no doubt
It's the place that integrates the house into society
That exposes us to neighbours with utmost propriety
When you sit on your front veranda you are there for all to see
It says, 'I've done my chores, stepped from my floor, come and talk me'
Why don't new houses have a front veranda, or verandas of any kind?
We have patios, entertaining areas and conservatories
As well as decks and decking and the outdoor blind
Hidden down the back, away from neighbours' eyes
What happened to the veranda, why was it put to sleep?
Why did it slip so much from grace, become almost obsolete?
I reckon I know when it happened, it was 1956
The Olympic games came to town and TV joined the mix

EVERY PERSON HAS A STORY

If every person has a story
How will we know how it ends?
If every person's life is a story
The ending will be known only by his friends
We know not when life will be complete
When the beginning, the middle and the end will meet
It could be today, it could be tomorrow
It could end in peace, it could end in sorrow
There may be end pieces that need to be tied
And that won't be done until we have died
Life whizzes by so fast
You can never change the past
So live your life and let it unfold
Wait 'til the end, then your story can be told

GRANDMOTHER

The kids have grown
My seeds well and truly sown
In the children who belong to me
We begin and end with the family
Doors to the future and the voices from the past
A family without history is wind through the grass
Now the real joy has begun
I really thought my work was done
Until I was gifted my precious grandson
A child to play and seek and hide with
To swing and jump and laugh and slide with
My heart swells up and my spirit de-wrinkles
I love this toddler with his cute dimples
Whose genes I share
And for whom I so fondly care
A snuggle and a book and a game
Surprises that make life fun again
If the truth be frankly told
Being Nanny is nature's gift for growing old

WE ARE ALL DYING TO GO THERE

When in town there's one place I always like to go
A place where I am sure to find many people that I know
It's through the town and up the hill
Keep on over a crest, until
You reach the dead centre of our town
A place we go to when life runs down
The view is great but cold, stiff winds blow
Over the silent graveyard from the ocean below
I silently think of my parents, my sister and brothers
But as well as them, there are many others
There is David Arthur Maxwell, dad's only brother
And the sad resting place of his father and mother
My great grand-parents Robert Allen and Annie Carstairs
And my great, great, grand-parents are also at rest there
There's old Uncle Dave, cousin Peter and baby Hector as well
Grand aunts, cousins and uncles make numbers swell
All these are family but that's not the end
There are many people in this place that I once knew as friend
People who shared the space when we were very young
Who played games, laughed at jokes, spent long days in the sun
People who were important in the schoolyard days
Before we grew and left our homes and went our separate ways
Each time I heard from locals that one of them was here
I fondly remembered, said a prayer, shed a silent tear
But the sad truth is, when it's all boiled down
I know more people in this place than I now know in the town

TIME TO END THE ISOLATION

We've managed to flatten down the curve
So it's time to brace and summon up the nerve
To end our frustration with lonely isolation
And renew participation in old-fashioned socialization
It's time to release the lead we're tethered to
Return to the life we once knew
Before staying inside our door and not venturing out at all
Let's get commerce up and going, restart the money flowing
Regain economic regularity by standing in solidarity
To get the nation back on its feet, make the virus beat retreat
Let's send the kids back to school,
re-open the gym and swimming pool
Ensuring that everybody obeys the 1.5 metre rule
It's been an interesting experiment against a foe savage and virulent
Our leaders told us what to do and by and large we did it too
Calming the savage beast initially, at least
Time to release the chain that binds us
Step back and see where it finds us
Learn how to manage the damage, perhaps make it vanish
After all, we Aussies did better than the Italians, British,
Americans or the Spanish!

OTHER WORKS BY ELSIE JOHNSTONE

Available from Amazon and other outlets

Our Little Town, Growing Up in Lakes Entrance 2009
Around the Kitchen Table (stories & verse) 2012
Lover, Husband, Father, Monster - Books 1 & 2 2010
Lover, Husband, Father, Monster - The Aftermath 2015
Ma's Garden 2012
Rainbow Over Narre Warren 2014

www.ingramcontent.com/pod-product-compliance
Lightning Source LLC
Chambersburg PA
CBHW030303010526
44107CB00053B/1805